Will WORKS

GETTING TO KNOW SHAKESPEARE

WRITTEN BY

ELODY RATHGEN AND

PAULINE SCANLAN

TITLE

Book Name:	**WILLWORKS** – *Getting to know Shakespeare*
ISBN Number:	1-872365 85X
Published:	2003

AUTHORS

Elody Rathgen and Pauline Scanlan

ACKNOWLEDGEMENTS

The publishers wish to acknowledge the work of the following people in the various stages of publishing this resource.

Artwork:	Geraldine Sloane, Craig Mitchell
Designer:	Graphic Solutions
Editor:	Pauline Scanlan

PUBLISHERS

Carel Press Ltd, 4 Hewson Street, Carlisle
Tel: 01228 538928 Fax: 591816
info@carelpress.com
www.carelpress.com
www.shakespeareresources.com

COPYRIGHT

COPYING NOTICE

PRINTED BY

Ashford Colour Press

ENVIRONMENTAL INFORMATION

This book is printed on 100% recycled paper which is made from printed waste and is not re-bleached. Using recycled paper saves trees, water & energy while reducing air pollution & landfill.

Contents

Carel Press Carlisle,   www.carelpress.com

GETTING TO KNOW SHAKESPEARE

Carel Press Carlisle,   www.carelpress.com.

Introduction

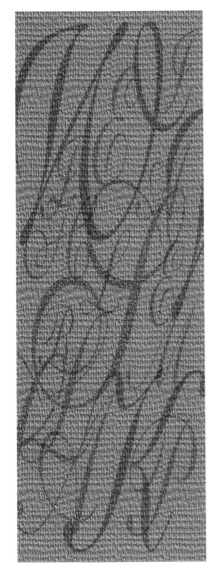

Recently, there has been renewed interest in introducing the works of Shakespeare to the general public. Film directors and actors from Britain, the United States and Australia have been jumping on the 'Bard's Bandwagon' to re-package, re-interpret, re-shape and re-invent a broad range of Shakespeare's works for a brand new audience – young people. If Shakespeare is working on the screen, it's up to us to make it work in the classroom.

Shakespeare wasn't always taught that well in the past. If we were lucky we might have come across a teacher who had a lively and enthusiastic approach to the Bard's work that captured our imaginations and laid the foundations for a love affair with Shakespeare's plays. If we were unlucky we came out of school thinking Shakespeare was a waste of time, irrelevant and too difficult.

Students shouldn't have to have a bad experience when they work with Shakespearian texts. The onus is on you, the teacher, to lay the foundations for that love affair. It's easy to teach Shakespeare badly. Just hand out copies of a play and start reading. It's not so easy to teach it well. To teach Shakespeare well takes time for planning. Time is in short supply these days in schools which is why we have written **Willworks**.

We can't teach Shakespeare for you, but we've taken time to look at a broad range of plays across three high interest areas:

• The Supernatural

• Crimes and Criminals

• Women in Shakespeare

We hope that the interesting and innovative approaches we suggest to working with snippets of text will give you a good spring board from which to launch any in-depth work on specific plays that you might be contemplating. If you are working with younger students see **Willworks** as providing them with a taste of joys to come. If you are working with senior students you will probably find material here that will link into whatever study you are planning, and it will also alert you to some new approaches to dealing with the texts.

• Elody Rathgen

• Pauline Scanlan

The Prologue

To be, or not to be – that is the question.

Get thee to a nunnery.

Once more unto the breach, dear friends, once more.

A horse! A horse! My kingdom for a horse!

What's in a name? That which we call a rose
By any other name would smell as sweet.

When shall we three meet again?
In thunder, lightning, or in rain?

Out, damned spot, out I say!

All the perfumes of Arabia will not sweeten
this little hand.

Go prick thy face and over-red thy fear,
Thou lily-livered boy.

All the world's a stage,
And all the men and women merely players.

From forth the fatal loins of these two foes
A pair of star-crossed lovers take their life.

FIND OUT

• *These quotations are some of Shakespeare's most famous lines. Do you know any others? See how many your class can come up with. Your teacher will help you out.*

• *How many of Shakespeare's play titles or characters do you know? Make another list.*

• *Prepare a wall display for your classroom during the time you are working on Willworks, and fill it with things about Shakespeare. Put up the names of characters, plays, lines you like, memorable phrases, jokes, insults, unusual Shakespearian words and other bits and pieces about the life and times of William Shakespeare. Make a brilliant display of your findings. Keep all this information up in your classroom. As you discover more about Shakespeare, add to your display. Check out film and play reviews too.*

Carel Press Carlisle,   www.carelpress.com.

Probably everyone in your class will have heard the name William Shakespeare. If you had to brainstorm something about him, you might be surprised how much information you already know about him and his work.

However, we must remember that William Shakespeare was born in England 400 years ago, towards the end of the 16th century. He was a playwright living in Tudor times. Yes, he has achieved great fame and recognition throughout history, and across many cultures. But all cultures have their great artists: writers, storytellers, thinkers, painters and so on. How many different cultures are represented in your classroom? Why not make it a class project to see how many other well known writers, storytellers, poets, playwrights and philosophers you can name from other cultures? You might have to ask at home for the names of these people. Collect as many names as you can. You could have a class list up on the wall. Which countries are these artists from? How many women's names are there?

THINK

Why don't you try a brainstorm out? Give everyone two minutes to think about anything that they associate with the name Shakespeare, and then share, on a large piece of paper, all the collective knowledge the class has about Shakespeare. Are you impressed by the amount they already know?

Carel Press Carlisle,   *www.carelpress.com*

Now...
welcome
to Act
One ...

Carel Press Carlisle,   www.carelpress.com.

ACT ONE

Supernatural Shakespeare

The Unexplained and the Mysterious

Supernatural Shakespeare

Do you have an interest in 'the unexplained'? You know, mysteries that no one seems to have found an answer to like the Bermuda Triangle, poltergeists or unidentified flying objects. You can probably think of lots more, and you might have your own strange stories to tell.

The curiosity that people have about these kinds of phenomena is not a new thing. For centuries, across all cultures, people have been fascinated by the possibility that there are elements of the world that cannot be explained by science or rational thought. This was certainly true in Shakespeare's day. Although Shakespeare was living at a time when science and discovery were making great leaps forward, for example, the first ships left England for America, the 'New World'. It was also a time when many people still looked at the world through fearful and superstitious eyes.

The infant mortality rate was high, the 'Black Death' was still rife in Europe and people's lives were short and often brutal. Most people were very religious with a strong belief in heaven and hell; they felt that they had little control over their own destiny. They placed themselves in the hands of Fate and Fortune. They looked to fortune tellers, sought out 'signs', followed astrology and heeded stories about the supernatural to help them make sense of their lives. You might think that not much has changed!

> **THINK**
>
> *Do you know people who read their 'stars' in magazines or who visit palm readers? Are you interested in that kind of thing yourself? If you are, do you know why?*

As an Elizabethan, the unexplained, the mysterious and the supernatural were certainly part of Shakespeare's life. He was knowledgeable about and interested in the supernatural world and the ways in which that world had an effect on both ordinary people and people of rank, like kings and queens. It's likely that he had his own superstitions and beliefs about the workings of the supernatural world that we would find surprising today.

ACT ONE

Supernatural Shakespeare

Ghosts, Fairies, and Soothsayers

Elements of the unexplained, the mysterious and the supernatural certainly found their way into many of Shakespeare's plays. To give you an idea, here is a selection of plays and some of the supernatural characters that appear in them:

Macbeth	three witches and a ghost
The Tempest	a magician and spirits
Antony and Cleopatra	a fortune-teller
A Midsummer Night's Dream	fairies and spirits
Hamlet	a ghost
Julius Caesar	a fortune-teller
Richard III	ghosts
Troilus and Cressida	a prophetess
Cymbeline	a fortune teller

GROUP WORK

In a small group talk about what uses these sorts of characters might have in a play. You don't need to know anything about the plays, you just need to keep in mind that Shakespeare included them for a purpose. Why might some have names and others not?

You'll notice that these characters mostly fall into three categories: ghosts, fairies and fortune tellers, or soothsayers. The ghosts and fairies (and also the witches in this case) belong in the realm of the supernatural; the fortune tellers (and the magician) can be classified as people with extraordinary powers. Some are named in the plays like Cobweb, Moth, Peaseblossom and Mustardseed in *A Midsummer Night's Dream*, other characters are not.

What kinds of thoughts did you have in your discussion group? You might have decided that the main purpose of the ghosts was to scare the living daylights out of the audience, or the other characters in the play, and you wouldn't be far wrong! However, many of these supernatural and mysterious characters also serve to provide 'other-worldly' warnings to the play's main characters, like the soothsayer in *Julius Caesar*.

Sometimes, they alert characters to wrongs that have been committed and that need to be put right, like the ghost in *Hamlet*. At other times they play tricks on characters to make them look foolish and teach them a lesson, or to give the audience a laugh, like the fairies and spirits in *A Midsummer Night's Dream*.

Carel Press Carlisle,   www.carelpress.com

Mysterious Quotations

ACT ONE

Supernatural Shakespeare

Below you will find some quotations which are related to the supernatural or mysterious from some of the plays we mentioned. In pairs, read them aloud, and see if you can work out if what is said is:

– a warning to someone

– said by someone who feels afraid

– to make someone feel guilty

– to stir someone into revenge

– to make someone look silly

■ Fetch me that flower, the herb I showed thee once.
The juice of it on sleeping eyelids laid
Will make or man or woman madly dote
Upon the next live creature that it sees...
... Having once this juice,
I'll watch Titania when she is asleep,
And drop the liquor of it in her eyes.
The next thing then she waking looks upc
Be it lion, bear, or wolf, or bull,
On meddling monkey, or on busy ape,
She shall pursue it with the soul of love.
(from A Midsummer Night's Dream)

■ Hence, horrible shadow!
Unreal mockery, hence!
(from Macbeth)

■ Let me sit heavy on thy soul tomorrow...
Think how thou stabbest me in my prime of youth
At Tewkesbury. Despair, therefore, and die!
(from Richard III)

■ If thou dost play with him at any game
Thou art sure to lose;
(from Antony & Cleopatra)

■ The serpent that did sting thy father's life
Now wears his crown.
(from Hamlet)

ACT OUT

Speak the lines in a way that helps convey the meaning of the words. So, for example, if you decide one of the examples is meant as a warning, you might speak the words slowly and deliberately.

Carel Press Carlisle,   www.carelpress.com

ACT ONE

Supernatural Shakespeare

Premonitions, Fate, and Strange Occurrences

Do you know what a premonition is? Have you ever had a sense that you knew something was going to happen? Perhaps you have had a dream that came true. Or you can sense when the telephone is about to ring. Shakespeare's characters often have premonitions, usually of a bad thing that's going to happen to them. If you have seen a performance of *Romeo and Juliet*, either on film, video or on the stage you will know that the story ends tragically. Both Romeo and Juliet die unnecessarily. If you were listening to the story very carefully as you watched you will have noticed that their impending deaths were signalled to the audience on several occasions throughout the play. For example, when Romeo is on his way to the Capulet's ball, where he meets Juliet for the first time, he has a sudden premonition of what is to come, and although he quickly forgets about it, the audience doesn't.

Benvolio This wind you talk of blows us from ourselves.
Supper is done, and we shall come too late.

Romeo I fear too early, for my mind misgives
Some consequences yet hanging in the stars
Shall bitterly begin his fearful date
With this night's revels, and expire the term
Of a despised life, closed in my breast,
By some vile forfeit of untimely death.

(Act 1, Scene 4)

THINK

If you were on your way to a party with a large group of your friends, and you were worried that something bad could possibly happen there, would you still go to the party? Discuss this idea with a small group.

Premonitions, Fate, and Strange Occurrences (cont.)

ACT ONE

Supernatural Shakespeare

Again, later in the play, Romeo secretly marries Juliet but he gets into a fight with Tybalt, Juliet's cousin, on his way back from the church and kills him. For this crime the Prince of Verona banishes Romeo to another city. Romeo and Juliet manage to spend a secret night together before he has to get out of town. As Romeo leaves Juliet's bedroom and climbs over the balcony to the garden below she seems to have a vision of his death, and says:

> **Juliet** O God, I have an ill-divining soul!
> Methinks I see thee, now thou art so low,
> As one dead in the bottom of a tomb.
> Either my eyesight fails, or thou look'st pale.

Romeo replies:

> **Romeo** And trust me, love, in my eye so do you.
> **(Act 3, Scene 5)**

ACT OUT

Read these lines aloud with another person. Imagine that you are saying goodbye to someone you love very much (it might be a relative or a friend) when you have a sudden fear that you might never see them again. In pairs write and then perform a 'leave-taking' scene where you show your concern for their leaving, but without making them feel as though they aren't able to go. Choose an appropriate setting and choose your words carefully. Be subtle, rather than overly dramatic. Don't try to copy Shakespeare's style. Use your own language.

Carel Press Carlisle,   www.carelpress.com

ACT ONE

Supernatural Shakespeare

Clarence's Dream

In *Richard lll*, the Duke of Clarence, brother of the Duke of Gloucester who later becomes King Richard, is imprisoned in the Tower of London. Here is the story he tells to his guard (his Keeper) after a terrible nightmare. Read it aloud in pairs:

Keeper   Why looks your Grace so heavily to-day?

Clarence   O, I have passed a miserable night,
So full of fearful dreams, of ugly sights,
That, as I am a Christian faithful man,
I would not spend such another night
Though 'twere to buy a world of happy days,
So full of dismal terror was the time!

Keeper   What was your dream, my lord? I pray you, tell me.

Clarence   Methoughts that I had broken from the Tower
And was embarked to cross to Burgundy,
And in my company my brother Gloucester,
Who from my cabin tempted me to walk
Upon the hatches; there we looked towards England,
And cited up a thousand heavy times,
During the wars of York and Lancaster,
That had befall'n us. As we paced along
Upon the giddy footing of the hatches,
Methought that Gloucester stumbled, and in falling
Struck me – that sought to stay him – overboard
Into the tumbling billows of the main.
O Lord, methought what pain it was to drown,
What dreadful noise of waters in my ears,
What sights of ugly death within my eyes!
Methoughts I saw a thousand fearful wrecks,
Ten thousand men that fishes gnawed upon,
Wedges of gold, great anchors, heaps of pearl,
Inestimable stones, unvalued jewels,
All scattered in the bottom of the sea.
Some lay in dead men's skulls, and in the holes

hatches = the deck

Where eyes did once inhabit, there were crept –
As 'twere in scorn of eyes – reflecting gems,
That wooed the slimy bottom of the deep
And mocked the dead bones that lay
scattered by.
(Act I, Scene 4)

In Clarence's dream he imagines ("methought") that his evil brother, the Duke of Gloucester, stumbles into him on the deck of a ship bound for France ("Burgundy") and knocks him into the sea, where he dies.

Soon after Clarence has told his dream to the guard he is set upon by two murderers who have been sent by his brother, Gloucester. They stab him and drown him in a vat of wine. In some productions he is shown as being drowned in his own bath. From this, you can probably see that the general feel of Clarence's premonition is correct, although the real circumstances are not the same as the dream. His actual death is much less 'poetic', and more brutal. In his dream he even has time to look at sights beneath the ocean as he drowns! In reality, although he dies bravely, trying to argue his case rationally with the men who come to kill him, his is a very ugly and 'ignoble' end.

ACT ONE

Supernatural Shakespeare

DESIGN WORK

Look back through Clarence's dream and highlight the parts of the dream that might be well represented as visual images.

Then consider how Clarence actually dies (if you want to read this part of the play for yourselves look at Act 1 Sc.4). Design a large image on A3 paper which shows the differences and similarities between the dream and the reality of Clarence's death. You might make the image multimedia and even include words from the scene to draw out the differences and similarities.

Carel Press Carlisle,   www.carelpress.com

ACT ONE

Supernatural Shakespeare

Written in the Stars

Although Shakespeare makes us aware, through his characters, that he was familiar with the beliefs of the times he does not indicate his own point of view on these matters. It is not uncommon for characters in his plays to present contradictory arguments. For example, at the very start of *Romeo and Juliet*, the Prologue sets out the whole course of the story for us:

> From forth the fatal loins of these two foes
> A pair of star-crossed lovers take their life,

Here the words "star-crossed lovers" show that the fate of the two lovers is somehow tied up with the stars, or astrology. In other words, the fate of the pair has already been sealed by a force beyond their control. However, Edmund, in *King Lear*, mocks astrology and the unreliability of its predictions:

Edmund   This is the excellent foppery of the world, that when we are sick in fortune, often the surfeits of our own behaviour, we make guilty of our disasters the sun, the moon, and stars...
(Act 1, Scene 2)

THINK

As a class consider the idea that our destinies are 'already written'. By this we mean that our futures have already been 'planned'; that all we need to do is to play a part in the drama of our lives as they unfold, and from time to time we might get a look, like Clarence in his dream, at what's in store for us. Where do individuals in the class stand on this idea? Are our destinies already "hanging in the stars" from the day we are born; or do we play a part in the shaping of our own futures?

Carel Press Carlisle,   www.carelpress.com

The 'Weird Sisters'

The play in which Shakespeare brings together a whole raft of supernatural forces and strange occurrences is *Macbeth*. Set in the dark and forbidding Scottish highlands, it tells the story of a great Scottish warrior, Macbeth, who is stopped by three witches as he makes his way home from a battle. They prophesy that he will become King of Scotland. Macbeth goes on to ensure that the prophecy comes true by murdering his way to the top job. The audience is left to ponder whether Macbeth would have become king if he had never met the witches and been driven to murder by his own ambition and impatience.

The witches in the story are intended to be very fearsome. Unlike the sprites and fairies found in other plays (who are often meddlesome and mischievous, but not malevolent), these characters are full of treachery and evil. During the years in which Shakespeare was writing, belief in witches was common, especially in rural places. If children were born with deformities, or crops failed, people sometimes looked to unusual or 'different' people in their communities for the cause. For example, women who lived alone were a prime target. These people were reviled and often put to death. Most were completely harmless.

With the three witches who open up the first scene in *Macbeth*, Shakespeare tapped into the deep-seated fears of many uneducated Elizabethan playgoers. There is nothing comfortable or homely about these three women. In the opening scene, their rhymes and incantations are accompanied by thunder and lightning. They meet on deserted moorland, and in caves. Their craft is dark and their words are tinged with hints of their associations with other-worldly beings, "our masters". Their supernatural powers anchor the progress of the story.

PRODUCTION ACTIVITY

Look at this scene from Act 4 in the play. Macbeth has already killed the king and been pronounced king himself. But he is afraid that his success and security might be short-lived. He visits the witches to ask what is in store for him in the future. So far, to try and secure his position as king, he has also murdered one of his most loyal soldiers, Banquo.

When he finds the witches, in a cave, they are expecting him and have been preparing a cauldron of unspeakable ingredients to use in a spell. On stage or on film this can be one of the most terrifying scenes in the play.

Carel Press Carlisle, www.carelpress.com

ACT ONE

Supernatural Shakespeare

READ THROUGH

With your teacher, read through the scene. Before you talk about it write down what you think is happening. Also make a note of any lines you had difficulty following. After this, as a class, discuss the points you made and questions you had.

• In groups give out the following parts:

Macbeth
_____

First Witch
_____

Second Witch
_____

Third Witch
_____

First Apparition (a head encased in armour)
_____

Second Apparition (a child covered in blood)
_____

Third Apparition (a child wearing a crown and holding a branch or small tree)
_____

Lennox (a lord who comes to find Macbeth)
_____

• Read through the scene again and, as you read, think about how you can create an atmosphere of fear and terror (for the audience) in your use of language. Try to make each part seem different and don't fall into the trap of 'hamming it up'. Next, walk through the part and make some decisions about how you would stage it. Make a note of these decisions. You need to think about the audience all the time. Firstly, ensuring that they can hear and understand what you say, secondly about how you will be positioned so that they can see and hear what is happening.

Second Witch	By the pricking of my thumbs, Something wicked this way comes. Open, locks, whoever knocks! *[Enter Macbeth]*
Macbeth	How now, you secret, black, and midnight hags, What is't you do?

ACT ONE

*S*upernatural *S*hakespeare

All	A deed without a name.
Macbeth	I conjure you by that which you profess,
	Howe'er you come to know it, answer me:
	Though you untie the winds and let them fight
	Against the churches, though the yeasty waves
	Confound and swallow navigation up,
	Though bladed corn be lodged and trees blown down,
	Though castles topple on their warders' heads,
	Though palaces and pyramids do slope
	Their heads to their foundations, though the treasure
	Of nature's germens tumble all together,
	Even till destruction sicken, answer me
	To what I ask you.
First Witch	Speak.
Second Witch	Demand.
Third Witch	We'll answer.
First Witch	Say, if thou'dst rather hear it from our mouths,
	Or from our masters?
Macbeth	Call 'em, let me see 'em.
First Witch	Pour in sow's blood, that hath eaten
	Her nine farrow; grease that's sweaten
	From the murderer's gibbet throw
	Into the flame.
All	Come, high or low,
	Thyself and office deftly show.

[Thunder. First Apparition: an armed head]

Macbeth	Tell me, thou unknown power –
First Witch	He knows thy thought:
	Hear his speech, but say thou nought.

germens = seeds of life

Carel Press Carlisle,   www.carelpress.com

ACT ONE

Supernatural Shakespeare

First Apparition	Macbeth, Macbeth, Macbeth, beware Macduff; Beware the Thane of Fife. Dismiss me. Enough.

[The apparition disappears]

Macbeth	Whate'er thou art, for thy good caution, thanks; Thou hast harped my fear aright: but one word more –
First Witch	He will not be commanded. Here's another, More potent than the first.

[Thunder. Second Apparition: A bloody child]

Second Apparition	Macbeth, Macbeth, Macbeth.
Macbeth	Had I three ears I'd hear thee.
Second Apparition	Be bloody, bold, and resolute. Laugh to scorn The power of man, for none of woman born Shall harm Macbeth.

[The apparition disappears]

Macbeth	Then live, Macduff – what need I fear of thee? But yet I'll make assurance double sure, And take a bond of fate thou shalt not live, That I may tell pale-hearted fear it lies, And sleep in spite of thunder.

[Thunder. Third Apparition: a child crowned, with a tree in his hand]

	What is this That rises like the issue of a king, And wears upon his baby-brow the round And top of sovereignty?
All	Listen, but speak not to't.

Carel Press Carlisle,   www.carelpress.com

ACT ONE

Supernatural Shakespeare

Third Apparition Be lion-mettled, proud, and take no care
Who chafes, who frets, or where conspirers are.
Macbeth shall never vanquish'd be until
Great Birnam Wood to high Dunsinane Hill
Shall come against him.

[The apparition disappears]

Macbeth   That will never be
Who can impress the forest, bid the tree
Unfix his earth-bound root? Sweet bodements! Good!
Rebellious dead, rise never till the wood
Of Birnam rise, and our high-placed Macbeth
Shall live the lease of nature, pay his breath
To time and mortal custom. Yet my heart
Throbs to know one thing. Tell me, if your art
Can tell so much, shall Banquo's issue ever
Reign in this kingdom?

All   Seek to know no more.

Macbeth   I will be satisfied. Deny me this,
And an eternal curse fall on you! Let me know.
Why sinks that cauldron? And what noise is this?

First Witch Show!

Second Witch   Show!

Third Witch Show!

All   Show his eyes, and grieve his heart;
Come like shadows, so depart.

[A show of eight kings, the last with a mirror in his hand; Ghost of Banquo following]

Macbeth   Thou art too like the spirit of Banquo. Down!
Thy crown does sear mine eyeballs. And thy hair,
Thou other gold-bound brow, is like the first.
A third is like the former. Filthy hags,

Carel Press Carlisle,   www.carelpress.com

ACT ONE

Supernatural Shakespeare

PRODUCTION

If you were preparing this scene to produce at a drama festival how would you deal with staging, costuming and the need for special effects? You might like to annotate (write notes alongside) this scene, design a stage set on paper with annotations, or build a small model of the set and write accompanying notes.

Why do you show me this? – A fourth? Start, eyes!
What, will the line stretch out to the crack of doom?
Another yet? A seventh? I'll see no more:
And yet the eighth appears, who bears a glass
Which shows me many more; and some I see
That two-fold balls and treble sceptres carry.
Horrible sight! Now I see 'tis true,
For the blood-boltered Banquo smiles upon me,
And points at them for his.

[Apparitions vanish]

What, is this so?

First Witch Ay, sir, all this is so: but why
Stands Macbeth thus amazedly?
Come, sisters, cheer we up his sprites,
And show the best of our delights.
I'll charm the air to give a sound,
While you perform your antic round
That this great king may kindly say,
Our duties did his welcome pay.

[Music. The witches dance and then vanish]

Macbeth Where are they? Gone? Let this pernicious hour
Stand aye accursed in the calendar.
Come in, without there!

[Enter Lennox]

Lennox What's your grace's will?

Macbeth Saw you the weird sisters?

Lennox No, my lord.

Macbeth Came they not by you?

Lennox No, indeed, my lord.

Macbeth Infected be the air whereon they ride,
And damned all those that trust them.

(Act 4, Scene 1)

23

Writing the Scenery

One of the things that Shakespeare had to do in his plays was actually describe the scenery, the weather and the time of day, because in his time, theatres could not provide all the special effects to show the audience what was happening. There was no lighting, of course, no sound system, and very little scenery was able to be put on stage. Sometimes a throne would be used to show that the scene was in a palace.

In *Hamlet* for example, Shakespeare used some interesting descriptions to give us an idea of the time of day. Look at the end of Act 1, Scene 1 where some guards who have been on duty all night know that the end of their watch has come when one says:

> But look, the morn in russet mantle clad
> Walks o'er the dew of yon high eastern hill.

Try to put this description of dawn breaking in your own language.

Here is another quotation from *Hamlet*:

> 'Tis now the very witching time of night,
> When churchyards yawn, and hell itself breathes out
> Contagion to this world. Now could I drink hot blood,
> And do such bitter business as the day
> Would quake to look on.
> *(Act 3, Scene 2)*

How vivid this description is! What time does it describe?
What do the different images mean to you?

Supernatural Shakespeare

WRITE AND DESIGN

Now, choose a time of day that you enjoy and try to write two or three sentences describing it without actually saying the hour. Use lively, imaginative and expressive language as Shakespeare has. Read your sentences out to each other and see if people can tell what time you mean. How accurate are they? Later, you might put these descriptions on larger sheets of paper, perhaps with some design work to set them off, and then display them around the wall. Shakespeare's examples could go on display too.

Carel Press Carlisle,   www.carelpress.com

ACT TWO

Crimes and Criminals

Murder, Mayhem and Revenge

ACT TWO

Crimes and Criminals

Among some of the most popular entertainments today are crime and police stories. Whether as books, television series, or films – detective, 'mysteries', suspense and crime-solving stories attract huge audiences.

What do people enjoy about such programmes or stories? Is it the excitement of trying to guess who did it (or who dunnit..)? Or is it a sense of interest in people getting justice? What other reasons could there be? Share as many as you can around your group. You might do a survey as a class to find out why people enjoy these kinds of stories so much.

In the best of these programmes, the ones people in your class have said they enjoy, what are the things that make them so enjoyable? Draw up a table to show the most common factors in successful crime dramas.

Since the times of Seneca, a Latin playwright from 4 B.C. – 65 A.D., such writing has always been popular. What people enjoyed about crime stories in those days were the details of the crime itself, the nature of the criminal characters, the theme of revenge and the ways in which people, without realising it at first, became involved in the crime, or were tricked into being accomplices. Sometimes the crime was an act of revenge for a previous crime. Many of these early works focused on the bloodiness and violence of the crime acts. This is what people seemed to enjoy.

Is this different from or similar to your survey work on what people today look for in a successful mystery or crime story?

THINK

Name some of the most popular crime or police programmes, or writers, or characters. If you have some personal favourites, note them down as well.

Are there particular character 'types' that emerge in these stories? Can you identify them?

Carel Press Carlisle,   www.carelpress.com

ACT TWO

Crimes and Criminals

The Revenge Story

William Shakespeare had a very good sense of what audiences enjoyed, and during his time the revenge story was also popular. He often borrowed plot details from well known revenge and mystery stories which he knew would attract people, but then he added other material and developed his own ideas and characters to make new plays out of old favourites. The famous *Hamlet* is one of the best examples of a revenge story. Here is a brief outline:

> Hamlet's father, the King of Denmark, dies suddenly and somewhat mysteriously. Very soon after the funeral Hamlet's mother remarries. Her new husband is the former king's brother, Claudius. Hamlet is upset by the quick remarriage and in his distressed state sees (or, perhaps he imagines it) his father's ghost. He becomes convinced that Claudius is in fact the murderer of his father.
>
> He devises a plan to appear to be mad so that he can investigate the situation under cover. In this state he rejects his girlfriend, Ophelia, who goes mad and dies. He alienates her brother Laertes, one time his friend, who then plots with Claudius, who is by now king, to get rid of Hamlet. Although he has the evidence to denounce Claudius as the murderer of the former king, Hamlet delays taking action. This gives Claudius time to put his murderous schemes in place, and in a dramatic climax all the major characters die. Laertes and Hamlet are poisoned by a lethal concoction put on the tips of their swords for the duel, Hamlet's mother drinks a poisonous chalice of wine, meant for Hamlet not her, and in his dying moment Hamlet manages to fatally stab Claudius.

PRODUCTION ACTIVITY

In groups, take one aspect of the Hamlet story and plan a short scene around it, just a short 'take' of 2 or 3 minutes. You might give it a modern setting, or you might set it back in an earlier time. Since you have been given only the bare bones of Hamlet's story, you will have to add details which you make up yourself. You will need to think more about the characters as well to develop what they are like. Plan your scene, keeping in mind the ideas you have discussed about successful crime stories. Your scene might focus on what happens to Ophelia, or it might be a scene between Hamlet and his mother, or perhaps something about Claudius' plotting to kill Hamlet. You will also have ideas of your own for other scenes.

The Revenge Story (cont.)

Several films have been made of Shakespeare's play, *Hamlet*, including one starring Mel Gibson, another one with Kenneth Branagh, and another famous one with the actor Sir Laurence Olivier taking the leading role. Ask your teacher to show you some scenes from one of the films which are similar to the scenes you have developed, practised and performed in your class.

After you have enjoyed viewing the scenes, you could discuss what similarities and differences there are between your scenes and the ones in the film. One topic for the discussion might be the language Shakespeare uses. In addition to looking at some of the film scenes, ask your teacher to show you some copies of extracts from the scenes, so that you can read Shakespeare's language for yourselves. Some extracts are reproduced on pages 59-64. What are some differences that you notice compared with the language which you used in your scenes?

ACT TWO
Crimes and Criminals

WRITING GROUPS

A typical revenge story of the period contained these elements, all of which can be found in Hamlet:

- *a villain*
- *a complex plot*
- *a ghost*
- *a suffering heroine*
- *lust*
- *torture and poisoning*
- *madness*
- *a play within a play*
- *characters of high rank*
- *murders*
- *an uncertain 'revenger'*

Choose a number of these elements and work out an outline for your own revenge story.

Carel Press Carlisle,   www.carelpress.com

ACT TWO

Crimes and Criminals

Moral Dilemmas

Today we have very well defined justice systems which set out clearly not only what actions are criminal, but also what rights people have. We are very careful about what powers the police force can use, and about the rules under which lawyers should conduct their cases. Consideration has been given to what penalties should be handed down when someone is found guilty. There is a lot of emphasis on making sure the law is fair to everyone, no matter what age, or culture, whether they are rich or poor, man or woman. There are technological and scientific processes which can be used to track criminals, even when the evidence is hard to find, and the criminal very skilful.

But policing and the law have not always been as carefully monitored as they now are. In the past it was more difficult to find and track criminals, because there weren't such sophisticated technologies and international communications to catch them. On the other hand in the past, since people lived in much smaller towns and communities they knew each other better, so it was harder to be anonymous or to go unnoticed. Strangers or odd events were quickly noticed and discovered.

Our ideas about crime and justice, guilt, revenge and responsibility have always been the subject of much discussion and debate. Many cases remain unsolved, and many people found guilty of crimes continue to protest that they are innocent until the day of their deaths. There are many such famous cases in this country and overseas. You might take the opportunity with your teacher to read and investigate some of these famous stories. Keep an eye on your local newspaper for the current court proceedings.

Sometimes the idea of guilt and innocence is not easily determined. It might be easy to pronounce that someone committed an illegal act – but what of the circumstances surrounding that act? What if someone stole to feed their family; what if someone killed to protect themselves?

Carel Press Carlisle, www.carelpress.com

Moral Dilemmas (cont.)

Here are some discussion ideas which you might use in groups or as a class to begin considering as moral dilemmas. Moral dilemmas are problems which can be viewed from many different positions and which do not have easy answers. Maybe on some of these matters you will not be able to agree at all. As well as discussing them in groups you might use them for debate topics, or for pieces of thoughtful essay writing.

- What sorts of actions do we consider criminal? Are there occasions when those actions might not be considered criminal?

- What sorts of situations make one crime worse than another?

- Is it useful to rank crimes in order of seriousness? Can you agree on a list? If not, what are the reasons causing your disagreements?

- Would we call something a crime if everyone involved was partly guilty?

- If a person is 'made to do a crime' because someone else gives them wrong information, should they be held responsible for it?

- When should we try to stop a friend from committing a crime? When do we 'grass-up' a person who is a friend?

- Can the justice system itself sometimes be guilty of unfairness?

CLARIFYING SOME LANGUAGE

Before you read the scene following, discuss your understandings of these terms and expressions. Write some sentences using them to show how they can be used in the context of the law:

- the letter of the law

- the spirit of justice

- mercy

- judgement

- sentence

- pardon

In most societies the law is seen to be above influence. It is supposed to offer everyone a fair opportunity in a public setting to have justice done, to have 'their day in court'. Shakespeare's plays *The Merchant of Venice* and *Measure for Measure* both have themes which focus on the administration of justice and the consequences of how the sentences of the courts affect people's lives.

ACT TWO

Crimes and Criminals

ACT TWO

Crimes and Criminals

From The Merchant of Venice

The story so far:

Bassanio has had to borrow money from his friend Antonio, a wealthy Venetian merchant. Because Antonio's money is all tied up in a big commercial venture, he has no available cash, so he borrows money from a moneylender, Shylock, to help his friend out. Lending money, in those days, was not a reputable business and was often handled by members of the Jewish community. Shylock is well known as a difficult man who has made a lot of money from his unpopular business. He and Antonio have never been the best of friends. In their written agreement about the money to be lent, they state that if Antonio cannot repay the bond in time, Shylock will take a pound of flesh from Antonio by way of repayment.

Antonio is so sure of his business success he sees the unusual agreement as a bit of a joke. However in a disastrous turn of events Antonio's venture is delayed and he has no money to repay on the agreed date. Attempts are made, through the justice system, to get the agreement overturned but in the courtroom Shylock is unmovable about his right to his bond. Portia, who is engaged to Bassanio, is the lawyer attempting to change Shylock's mind. (She is, of course, in disguise as a young man, since women could not hold any public office in those days!) Her first appeal, in one of Shakespeare's most famous speeches, is to Shylock's sense of mercy. But he cannot be moved. She then turns to the 'letter of the law.'

Carel Press Carlisle,   *www.carelpress.com*

GETTING TO KNOW SHAKESPEARE

ACT TWO

Crimes and Criminals

CLARIFYING THE STORY

Some other things you need to know to help you follow and respond to the situation are that:

- Antonio and Shylock have a history of conflict, with Antonio being publicly critical of Shylock in the past for being a moneylender and charging interest.

- Shylock is a very proud Jewish man who has suffered abuse and racism from many people. He is brokenhearted that his daughter, Jessica, has run off with a Christian man, Lorenzo, to get married.

- Earlier in the play, Shylock has expressed his deep feelings about the way in which he is often caused to suffer at the hands of the Christians, and that he has learnt by their example to be hard-hearted. Here is the speech in which he explains how he has been harassed and mistreated by others:

Shylock: *(with reference to Antonio)*

He hath disgraced me, and hindered me half a million; laughed at my losses, mocked at my gains, scorned my nation, thwarted my bargains, cooled my friends, heated mine enemies, and what's his reason? – I am a Jew. Hath not a Jew eyes? Hath not a Jew hands, organs, dimensions, senses, affections, passions; fed with the same food, hurt with the same weapons, subject to the same diseases, healed by the same means, warmed and cooled by the same winter and summer as a Christian is? If you prick us do we not bleed? If you tickle us do we not laugh? If you poison us do we not die? And if you wrong us shall we not revenge? If we are like you in the rest, we will resemble you in that. If a Jew wrong a Christian, what is his humility? Revenge. If a Christian wrong a Jew, what should his sufferance be by Christian example? Why, revenge. The villainy you teach me I will execute, and it shall go hard but I will better the instruction.

(Act 3, Scene 1)

Carel Press Carlisle, www.carelpress.com

ACT TWO

Crimes and Criminals

THE COURT SCENE

Duke   You hear the learn'd Bellario, what he writes,

And here, I take it, is the doctor come.

[Enter Portia, dressed like a doctor of laws]

Give me your hand. Come you from old Bellario?

Portia   I did, my lord.

Duke   You are welcome, take your place.

Are you acquainted with the difference

That holds this present question in the court?

Portia   I am informed thoroughly of the cause.

Which is the merchant here, and which the Jew?

Duke   Antonio and old Shylock, both stand forth.

Portia   Is your name Shylock?

Shylock   Shylock is my name.

Portia   Of a strange nature is the suit you follow,

Yet in such rule that the Venetian law

Cannot impugn you as you do proceed.

You stand within his danger, do you not?

Antonio   Ay, so he says.

Portia   Do you confess the bond?

Antonio   I do.

Portia   Then must the Jew be merciful.

Shylock   On what compulsion must I? Tell me that.

Portia   The quality of mercy is not strained,

It droppeth as the gentle rain from heaven

Upon the place beneath: it is twice blest;

It blesseth him that gives and him that takes,

'Tis mightiest in the mightiest, it becomes

The throned monarch better than his crown.

His sceptre shows the force of temporal power,

impugn = criticise, challenge

ACT TWO

The attribute to awe and majesty,
Wherein doth sit the dread and fear of kings;
But mercy is above this sceptred sway;
It is enthroned in the hearts of kings,
It is an attribute to God himself,
And earthly power doth then show likest God's
When mercy seasons justice. Therefore, Jew,
Though justice be thy plea, consider this,
That, in the course of justice, none of us
Should see salvation: we do pray for mercy,
And that same prayer doth teach us all to render
The deeds of mercy. I have spoke thus much
To mitigate the justice of thy plea,
Which if thou follow, this strict court of Venice
Must needs give sentence 'gainst the merchant there.

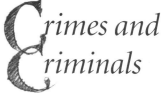

Crimes and Criminals

Shylock   My deeds upon my head! I crave the law,
            The penalty and forfeit of my bond.

Portia   Is he not able to discharge the money?

Bassanio Yes, here I tender it for him in the court,
            Yea, twice the sum – if that will not suffice,
            I will be bound to pay it ten times o'er,
            On forfeit of my hands, my head, my heart –
            If this will not suffice, it must appear
            That malice bears down truth. And I beseech you,
            Wrest once the law to your authority:
            To do a great right, do a little wrong,
            And curb this cruel devil of his will.

Portia   It must not be; there is no power in Venice
            Can alter a decree established:
            'Twill be recorded for a precedent,

Carel Press Carlisle,   www.carelpress.com

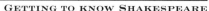
ACT TWO

Crimes and Criminals

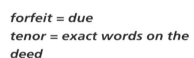

forfeit = due
tenor = exact words on the deed

	And many an error by the same example
	Will rush into the state. It cannot be.
Shylock	A Daniel come to judgement! Yea, a Daniel!
	O wise young judge, how I do honour thee!
Portia	I pray you let me look upon the bond.
Shylock	Here 'tis, most reverend doctor, here it is.
Portia	Shylock, there's thrice thy money offered thee.
Shylock	An oath, an oath, I have an oath in heaven.
	Shall I lay perjury upon my soul?
	No, not for Venice.
Portia	Why, this bond is forfeit,
	And lawfully by this the Jew may claim
	A pound of flesh, to be by him cut off
	Nearest the merchant's heart. Be merciful,
	Take thrice thy money, bid me tear the bond.
Shylock	When it is paid according to the tenor.
	It doth appear you are a worthy judge,
	You know the law, your exposition
	Hath been most sound: I charge you by the law,
	Whereof you are a well-deserving pillar,
	Proceed to judgement: by my soul I swear
	There is no power in the tongue of man
	To alter me – I stay here on my bond.
Antonio	Most heartily I do beseech the court
	To give the judgement.
Portia	Why then, thus it is:
	You must prepare your bosom for his knife.
Shylock	O noble judge! O excellent young man!
Portia	For the intent and purpose of the law
	Hath full relation to the penalty,
	Which here appeareth due upon the bond.
Shylock	'Tis very true: O wise and upright judge!
	How much more elder art thou than thy looks!

Carel Press Carlisle,   www.carelpress.com

ACT TWO

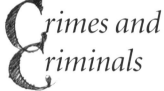

Crimes and Criminals

Portia	Therefore lay bare your bosom.
Shylock	Ay, his breast,
	So says the bond, doth it not, noble judge?
	"Nearest his heart," those are the very words.
Portia	It is so. Are there balance here to weigh
	The flesh?
Shylock	I have them ready.
Portia	Have by some surgeon, Shylock, on your charge,
	To stop his wounds, lest he do bleed to death.
Shylock	Is it so nominated in the bond?
Portia	It is not so expressed, but what of that?
	'Twere good you do so much for charity.
Shylock	I cannot find it, 'tis not in the bond.
Portia	You, merchant, have you any thing to say?
Antonio	But little. I am armed and well prepared.
	Give me your hand, Bassanio, fare you well!
	Grieve not that I am fallen to this for you;
	For herein Fortune shows herself more kind
	Than is her custom: it is still her use
	To let the wretched man outlive his wealth,
	To view with hollow eye and wrinkled brow
	An age of poverty; from which lingering penance
	Of such misery doth she cut me off.
	Commend me to your honourable wife,
	Tell her the process of Antonio's end,
	Say how I loved you, speak me fair in death;
	And, when the tale is told, bid her be judge
	Whether Bassanio had not once a love.
	Repent but you that you shall lose your friend,
	And he repents not that he pays your debt;
	For if the Jew do cut but deep enough,
	I'll pay it instantly with all my heart.

Carel Press Carlisle,   www.carelpress.com

ACT TWO

Crimes and Criminals

Bassanio	Antonio, I am married to a wife Which is as dear to me as life itself, But life itself, my wife, and all the world, Are not with me esteemed above thy life. I would lose all, ay, sacrifice them all Here to this devil, to deliver you.
Portia	Your wife would give you little thanks for that, If she were by to hear you make the offer.
Gratiano	I have a wife who I protest, I love – I would she were in heaven so she could Entreat some power to change this currish Jew.
Nerissa	'Tis well you offer it behind her back; The wish would make else an unquiet house.
Shylock	*[Aside]* These be the Christian husbands. I have a daughter – Would any of the stock of Barrabas Had been her husband rather than a Christian. We trifle time, I pray thee pursue sentence.
Portia	A pound of that same merchant's flesh is thine, The court awards it, and the law doth give it.
Shylock	Most rightful judge!
Portia	And you must cut this flesh from off his breast, The law allows it, and the court awards it.
Shylock	Most learned judge! A sentence! Come, prepare!
Portia	Tarry a little; there is something else. This bond doth give thee here no jot of blood: The words expressly are "a pound of flesh" Take then thy bond, take thou thy pound of flesh;

	But, in the cutting it, if thou dost shed
	One drop of Christian blood, thy lands and goods
	Are, by the laws of Venice, confiscate
	Unto the state of Venice.
Gratiano	O upright judge! Mark, Jew: O learned judge!
Shylock	Is that the law?
Portia	Thyself shalt see the act: For, as thou urgest justice, be assured Thou shalt have justice, more than thou desirest.
Gratiano	O learned judge! Mark, Jew: a learned judge!
Shylock	I take this offer, then; pay the bond thrice And let the Christian go.
Bassanio	Here is the money.
Portia	Soft! The Jew shall have all justice. Soft, no haste. He shall have nothing but the penalty.
Gratiano	O Jew! an upright judge, a learned judge!
Portia	Therefore prepare thee to cut off the flesh. Shed thou no blood, nor cut thou less nor more But just a pound of flesh. If thou tak'st more Or less than a just pound, be it but so much As makes it light or heavy in the substance, Or the division of the twentieth part Of one poor scruple, nay, if the scale do turn But in the estimation of a hair, Thou diest, and all thy goods are confiscate.
Gratiano	A second Daniel, a Daniel, Jew! Now, infidel, I have you on the hip.
Portia	Why doth the Jew pause? Take thy forfeiture.
Shylock	Give me my principal, and let me go.

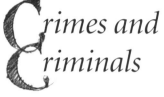

Crimes and Criminals

Carel Press Carlisle,   www.carelpress.com

ACT TWO

Crimes and Criminals

Bassanio	I have it ready for thee. Here it is.
Portia	He hath refused it in the open court:
	He shall have merely justice and his bond.
Gratiano	A Daniel, still say I, a second Daniel!
	I thank thee, Jew, for teaching me that word.
Shylock	Shall I not have barely my principal?
Portia	Thou shalt have nothing but the forfeiture
	To be so taken at thy peril, Jew.
Shylock	Why, then the devil give him good of it!
	I'll stay no longer question.
Portia	Tarry, Jew,

The law hath yet another hold on you.
It is enacted in the laws of Venice,
If it be proved against an alien
That by direct or indirect attempts
He seek the life of any citizen,
The party 'gainst the which he doth contrive
Shall seize one half his goods; the other half
Comes to the privy coffer of the state,
And the offender's life lies in the mercy
Of the Duke only, 'gainst all other voice.
In which predicament I say thou stand'st,
For it appears by manifest proceeding,
That indirectly, and directly too,
Thou hast contrived against the very life
Of the defendant; and thou hast incurred
The danger formerly by me rehearsed.
Down therefore, and beg mercy of the Duke.
(Act 4, Scene 1)

ACT TWO

Crimes and Criminals

PRODUCTION ACTIVITY

Once you have read this extract, predict the outcomes of the scene. Then consider some of the production elements needed to make it successful for an audience to watch. With your teacher's help, set up the classroom as a formal courtroom, and choose a cast to perform the scene. Divide into groups, each group focusing on a different aspect of the production. One group, for example, could consider costume, another the courtroom setting; smaller groups could each take one of the main characters and give the actors advice on how to present their characters. There might be other production factors for people to consider as well. Try to complete the scene in your own words and then look at how it really ended.

How would the media have handled the event? Write a headline and opening sentence for your local newspaper, or the opening lines of your local television station's report, or the opening questions in a radio interview with Antonio, or Shylock, or Portia immediately after the court's decision had been announced.

THINK

After the performance, discuss what issues the production has brought out in relation to themes and character portrayal. For example:

– consider who gains the audience's sympathy

– has the court been fair?

– have we seen 'the letter of the law' in operation, or 'the spirit of justice'?

– has justice been done?

Carel Press Carlisle,   www.carelpress.com

ACT TWO

Crimes and Criminals

From Measure for Measure

This play revolves around the contrasts which exist sometimes between people's public and private lives. In this play a wise duke is aware that his city needs some reforming, especially some tightening up on moral issues. For example, he thinks that prostitution in the city should be cleared up, and various other things as well. He fears that he may not be the right person to deal with the problems, so he goes on leave for some weeks leaving his deputy Angelo, who is a very 'hard line' sort of person, in charge.

Angelo begins the task, part of which includes arresting two citizens, Claudio and Juliet, who have conceived a child 'out of wedlock'. Claudio's friends get together to help him, and decide that the best person to approach Angelo to ask for his mercy would be Claudio's sister, Isabella, who is about to enter a convent. They think her innocence will make a good impression on Angelo. It does! In fact so much so that Angelo falls in love with her and tries to persuade her to have an affair with him. In return he says he will release Claudio.

Isabella is shocked and refuses, much to everyone's amazement. Great pressure is put on her to change her mind. Other 'murky' details emerge about Angelo's past as well and Claudio's life looks very much under threat. In a surprising twist, the original Duke returns in disguise to discover what is going on. With Isabella's help, though not without risk to various people, he is finally able to expose Angelo and return to his rightful place.

You and your teacher might like to look at some extracts (particularly Act 1 Scene 2) from *Measure for Measure*. (See page 42 for a short extract.) In fact in many of Shakespeare's plays, especially the ones called tragedies, separating out those who are guilty and those who are innocent is extremely difficult and causes many hours of discussion and debate. There are crimes done 'for the good of someone or something', personal crimes, political crimes, and many others. You will find all this out as you experience more of Shakespeare's plays, either in stage performances, films, or class readings.

THINK

Many more moral dilemmas arise in this play:

– should Isabella sacrifice herself for her brother's life?

– Claudio is guilty under the laws of the city, should he expect his sister to do this for him?

– the Duke's abandonment of his people leaves them in the hands of a ruthless and corrupt man. Should he have left them? Why didn't he take the responsibility himself to clean up the city? Why did he want someone else to do his dirty work?

– when people are in public positions, should their own private lives be under public scrutiny?

MEASURE FOR MEASURE

The scene begins with Lucio and two gentleman joking with each other about the consequences of their sexual habits and continues with a brothel-keeper bemoaning the fact that all their establishments in the suburbs would be closed down because of the Duke's proclamation.

Then Claudio is brought in by a guard and takes the chance to explain his situation and appeal for help.

Claudio	Thus stands it with me. Upon a true contract,
	I got possession of Julietta's bed.
	You know the lady; she is fast my wife,
	Save that we do the denunciation lack
	Of outward order...
	But it chances
	The stealth of our most mutual entertainment
	With character too gross is writ on Juliet.
Lucio	With child, perhaps?
Claudio	Unhapp'ly even so.
	And the new deputy now for the Duke–...
	Awakes me all the enrollèd penalties
	Which have, like unscoured armour, hung by th' wall
	So long that fourteen zodiacs have gone round,
	And none of them been worn;...
	'Tis surely for a name.
Lucio	I warrant it is;
	Send after the Duke, and appeal to him.
Claudio	I have done so, but he's not to be found.
	I prithee, Lucio, do me this kind service.
	This day my sister should the cloister enter,
	And there receive her approbation.
	Acquaint her with the danger of my state.
	Implore her in my voice that she make friends
	To the strict deputy. Bid herself assay him.
	I have great hope in that, for in her youth
	There is a prone and speechless dialect
	Such as move men; beside, she hath prosperous art
	When she will play with reason and discourse,
	And well she can persuade.
Lucio	I pray she may–... I'll to her.
Claudio	I thank you, good friend Lucio.
Lucio	Within two hours.
Claudio	Come, officer; away.

Crimes and Criminals

Carel Press Carlisle, www.carelpress.com

ACT THREE

Women of Words

Challenging Convention

Women of Words

This section gives you an opportunity to look broadly at some of the 'women of words' Shakespeare presents to us. You will have a chance to speak their speeches and stage them, comment on the situations some of these women find themselves in and explore what you might do in such circumstances and, of course, gain an insight into why these parts are some of the most sought after in the world of theatre.

There's no doubt Shakespeare wrote good parts for women. Even though, when he wrote them, the women's parts were performed by boys! (The Kings' Men, Shakespeare's own production company, had, at any one time, only five or six boys on its payroll. This probably accounts for the fact that there are fewer women's than men's parts in Shakespeare's plays.) Even so, the parts for women, like the parts for men, tend to be strong, challenging and complex.

Desdemona, Portia, Isabella, Lady Macbeth, Cordelia, Viola, Katherina, Beatrice, Cleopatra, Juliet, and Rosalind are some of the most famous Shakespearian women characters. How should we, today, view these Shakespearian women of the 16th century?

In Shakespeare's times, women had few of the opportunities that are possible today to take leadership roles, to have careers, to have any sort of education or occupation that took them away from the domestic spheres of living. However, in his plays Shakespeare has created many women characters who challenge the conventions of his time. True they usually have to be in disguise as men to do the unusual things, as we saw earlier on with the character of Portia in *The Merchant of Venice*.

Because she uses a disguise as a young male lawyer, Portia is not criticised for her actions. Portia is unusual in other ways in that she has control over her own financial and social life. Her father has died leaving her a very wealthy young woman. She is not dependent on anyone. She has her own house. She never needs to seek permission for what she does. Olivia, in *Twelfth Night* is another example of a woman able to exercise control over her own life because she has been left financially independent.

This is not true for all his women characters however, many of whom are dependent on other people for their livelihood. Even so, some of these women do act differently from the normal expected patterns for women of their time.

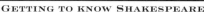
ACT THREE

Women of Words

From Romeo and Juliet

THE NURSE

Who looked after you when you were a baby? This might seem like a simple question, but it's actually quite complicated. According to your cultural background or the circumstances of your birth, you could have been looked after by any number of people other than your birth mother or father. Many babies are looked after by members of their extended family and others are looked after by a carer whilst their parents are at work. There will be lots of other possibilities too. Consider what your situation was. You do not have to discuss this with anyone else, though you might like to write about it.

In Shakespeare's times (and indeed this is still the case today in many wealthy families) it was not unusual for rich parents to give over the upbringing of their child to a nurse (today called a nanny). The woman would usually live with the family, or close by and would often breast-feed the child herself in its infancy (this is not now usual in wealthy families!). This person was known as a wet nurse. Today, the idea of someone other than the mother breast-feeding a child is virtually unheard of in western culture, but in the past it was a recognised form of employment for women.

You probably already know the story of *Romeo and Juliet*, and you might have seen the film version of the story by Baz Luhrmann in which the part of Juliet's nurse is played, hilariously, by Miriam Margolyles. You might also have seen an older film version of the story by Franco Zeffirelli. If you laughed as you watched Juliet's nurse in either of these versions, you will have some sense of Shakespeare's gift for drawing comic roles.

The Nurse is garrulous (talkative), she laughs at her own jokes, she is lewd and she also has a wonderful relationship with Juliet. (Don't forget that the Nurse brought Juliet up). The part of the Nurse is usually played by an older woman, sometimes a well-known comic actor, who has the stature and experience to bring such a role off. Her role is not just to make the audience laugh but also to act as a go-between for Juliet and Romeo and to highlight the more distant relationship that Juliet has with her parents.

In the scene on the next couple of pages the Nurse has visited Romeo in order to discover the arrangements for his secret marriage to Juliet. She returns with the news to Juliet, though she is exhausted from walking through the hot Italian sunshine. Juliet is bursting to hear what the arrangements are, but the Nurse, partly teasingly, partly through tiredness, makes her wait for the news.

PRODUCTION ACTIVITY

In groups of three take these three roles: director, Juliet, the Nurse. As a team work through the two speaking parts in the scene discussing them as you go. You might like to enlarge a copy of this exchange on A3 paper.

The director, in consultation with Juliet and the Nurse, should write notes and directions for movement and expression at each exchange. For example, Juliet has been waiting three hours for the nurse to return from what was supposed to be a half hour errand, so how is she likely to say her first lines? When Juliet says in frustration, "How art thou out of breath, when thou hast breath To say to me that thou art out of breath?" you might note that Juliet says this crossly and leans over the Nurse as she speaks.

You should try to show Juliet's mounting tensions and the Nurse's quiet enjoyment of keeping Juliet waiting. This scene is meant to be humorous for the audience, so keep this in mind as you discuss it.

Also remember:

– Juliet and the Nurse have a great deal of love for each other

– Juliet is very young and impatient

– the Nurse is concerned for Juliet's well-being.

There are several 'mood changes' in this exchange, so take care not to skip over them.

Juliet	Now, good sweet Nurse – O Lord, why look'st thou sad?
	Though news be sad, yet tell them merrily;
	If good, thou shamest the music of sweet news
	By playing it to me with so sour a face.
Nurse	I am a-weary, give me leave awhile.
	Fie, how my bones ache. What a jaunce have I had!
Juliet	I would thou hadst my bones, and I thy news:
	Nay, come, I pray thee, speak; good, good nurse, speak.
Nurse	Jesu, what haste! Can you not stay a while?
	Do you not see that I am out of breath?

jaunce = journey

Carel Press Carlisle,   www.carelpress.com

ACT THREE

Women of Words

Juliet	How art thou out of breath when thou hast breath
	To say to me that thou art out of breath?
	The excuse that thou dost make in this delay
	Is longer than the tale thou dost excuse.
	Is thy news good or bad? Answer to that.
	Say either, and I'll stay the circumstance.
	Let me be satisfied, is't good or bad?
Nurse	Well, you have made a simple choice. You know not how to choose a man. Romeo? No, not he; though his face be better than any man's, yet his leg excels all men's, and for a hand and a foot and a body, though they be not to be talked on, yet they are past compare. He is not the flower of courtesy, but, I'll warrant him, as gentle as a lamb. Go thy ways, wench, serve God. What, have you dined at home?
Juliet	No, no. But all this did I know before.
	What says he of our marriage? What of that?
Nurse	Lord, how my head aches! What a head have I!
	It beats as it would fall in twenty pieces.
	My back o' t' other side, – ah, my back, my back!
	Beshrew your heart for sending me about
	To catch my death with jaunting up and down!
Juliet	I' faith, I am sorry that thou art not well.
	Sweet, sweet, sweet Nurse, tell me, what says my love?
Nurse	Your love says, like an honest gentleman, and a courteous, and a kind, and a handsome, and, I warrant, a virtuous – Where is your mother?
Juliet	Where is my mother? Why, she is within;
	Where should she be? How oddly thou repliest!
	"Your love says, like an honest gentleman, Where is your mother?"

Carel Press Carlisle,   www.carelpress.com

ACT THREE

omen of
ords

Nurse	O God's lady dear!
	Are you so hot? Marry, come up, I trow.
	Is this the poultice for my aching bones?
	Henceforward do your messages yourself.
Juliet	Here's such a coil! Come, what says Romeo?
Nurse	Have you got leave to go to shrift to-day?
Juliet	I have.
Nurse	Then hie you hence to Friar Laurence cell.
	There stays a husband to make you a wife.
	Now comes the wanton blood up in your cheeks.
	They'll be in scarlet straight at any news.
	Hie you to church. I must another way,
	To fetch a ladder, by the which your love
	Must climb a bird's nest soon when it is dark.
	I am the drudge and toil in your delight,
	But you shall bear the burden soon at night.
	Go, I'll to dinner. Hie you to the cell.
Juliet	Hie to high fortune! Honest Nurse, farewell.

(Act 2, Scene 6)

marry come up, I trow = by the Virgin Mary, wait a moment I trust
(This is an expression of irritation)

shrift = to go to confession

THINK, WRITE AND DESIGN

• *Try casting a boy as the Nurse. What difference does this make to the part?*

• *Make up the scene which might follow this. Imagine that the Nurse is having a chat with the cook of the Capulet household. During the chat she talks about her meeting with Romeo, her thoughts about Juliet's secret marriage and why she took her time telling Juliet the news. Make the scene humorous. Use your own language.*

• *Design the kind of costume that you think the Nurse might have worn on her errand to Romeo (she would have been wanting to look her best) and then look at Act 2 Scene 4, lines 82-88 in the play.*

ACT THREE

Women of Words

From Antony and Cleopatra

CLEOPATRA

The story of *Antony and Cleopatra* is one of the most famous love stories of all time, and it's also true. Set against the backdrop of ancient Egypt it is a grand story of exotic passion! You might even have seen it famously brought to the screen by Richard Burton and Elizabeth Taylor. It's definitely worth having a look at part of this old movie to get a feel for the 'scale' of this story. Why is it so grand and full of passion? Mainly because of the location – Egypt, and the reputation of its fiery heroine – Cleopatra.

THINK AND WRITE

What do you already know about ancient Egypt? Brainstorm everything you know on the board with your class. At this stage it will probably just be odd words and images. Next brainstorm any questions you have about this period of history. Then add any details you know about the historical figure, Cleopatra. Can anyone else in the class answer the questions which have come up? Spend some time in the library seeing if you can extend your knowledge of this period and finding out about Cleopatra.

When Shakespeare decided to turn this story into a play, it was already a well-known tale. He would have got the story from a famous Greek book called *Parallel Lives* – the author was Plutarch (AD c.46-126), a writer and philosopher. Rather like many screen writers today, Shakespeare got most of his stories from already 'available sources' rather than making up the stories himself. You have probably seen many films that have been adapted from novels. Well, Shakespeare adapted written works in this way for his plays–not all the plays, of course–but you will find, if you research the lives of some of the famous people he wrote about, that the stories are factually correct. So, he took the factual story and invented other characters who add to the plot and themes, created motives and compacted the 'life and times' of whoever into a two or three hour stage play. This is what he does with Mark Antony and Queen Cleopatra who really did have a love affair that, centuries ago, led to their demise.

ACT THREE

*W*omen of *W*ords

HOW DID THEY MEET?

This is not a typical boy-meets-girl story. In fact, by the time Antony and Cleopatra got together, Antony had been married five times (though Shakespeare conveniently ignores this!) The love story is set in the time of the Roman Empire. At this time a large portion of the known world was administered by the Romans and divided into a number of parts. Each part was administered by a Roman general. Mark Antony had the Eastern Mediterranean as his responsibility and this is how he came to meet the most famous queen of Egypt, Cleopatra.

Much has been made of how involved the soldier, Mark Antony, was with this exotic queen. Even the history books show that he cared less and less about his role as a governor and more about his liaison with the queen as time went on. Shakespeare takes this theme of 'giving up everything for love' as the basis for the play he writes about them. He also focuses on the legendary beauty of Cleopatra and her fiery nature. It is Cleopatra's combination of beauty and fire which Shakespeare highlights as being both frightening and irresistible.

A FEARFUL BEAUTY

Shakespeare presents Cleopatra as a woman of many moods. She can be charming, cunning, funny, noble and angry within the space of a few scenes. But one constant that she does have is the ability to make people sit up and take notice. Look at the way she is described as she sits in the royal barge on a trip down the River Nile. Cleopatra clearly liked to make an impression!

> The barge she sat in, like a burnished throne,
> Burned on the water. The poop was beaten gold;
> Purple the sails, and so perfumed that
> The winds were love-sick with them. The oars were silver,
> Which to the tune of flutes kept stroke, and made
> The water which they beat to follow faster,
> As amorous of their strokes. For her own person,
> It beggared all description: she did lie
> In her pavilion – cloth-of-gold of tissue –
> O'er-picturing that Venus where we see
> The fancy outwork nature. On each side her

50

ACT THREE

Women of Words

Stood pretty dimpled boys, like smiling Cupids,
With divers-coloured fans, whose wind did seem
To glow the delicate cheeks which they did cool,
And what they undid did.
(Act 2, Scene 2)

READ THROUGH

Now read this next short extract which shows another side to Cleopatra's character. Here, a messenger comes with the news that, whilst on a trip back to Rome, Antony has married, for political reasons, Octavia, the sister of Caesar. Because the messenger is afraid of how she might react, he takes his time to break the news. By the time he tells her, in this extract, Cleopatra has worked herself into a frenzy of frustration.

Messenger Madam, he's married to Octavia.

Cleopatra   The most infectious pestilence upon thee!

[Strikes him down]

Messenger Good madam, patience.

Cleopatra   What say you? Hence,

[Strikes him again]

> Horrible villain, or I'll spurn thine eyes
> Like balls before me! I'll unhair thy head!

[She hales him up and down]

> Thou shalt be whipped with wire and stew'd in brine,
> Smarting in lingering pickle.

Messenger   Gracious madam,
I that do bring the news made not the match.

Cleopatra   Say 'tis not so, a province I will give thee,
And make thy fortunes proud. The blow thou hadst
Shall make thy peace for moving me to rage;
And I will boot thee with what gift beside
Thy modesty can beg.

ACT THREE

Women of Words

Messenger He's married, madam.

Cleopatra Rogue, thou hast lived too long.
[Draws a knife]

Messenger Nay then, I'll run...
[Exit]
(Act 2, Scene 5)

Later, Cleopatra sends the same messenger to see what Octavia is like. He comes back, some time later, with this report. Note how he has learned his lesson! Charmian is Cleopatra's handmaid.

Cleopatra Didst thou behold Octavia?

Messenger Ay, dread queen.

Cleopatra   Where?

Messenger   Madam, in Rome;
I looked her in the face, and saw her led
Between her brother and Mark Antony.

Cleopatra Is she as tall as me?

Messenger She is not, madam.

Cleopatra Didst hear her speak? Is she shrill-tongued or low?

Messenger Madam, I heard her speak. She is low-voiced.

Cleopatra That's not so good. He cannot like her long.

Charmian Like her? O Isis, 'tis impossible!

Cleopatra I think so, Charmian. Dull of tongue, and dwarfish!
What majesty is in her gait? Remember,
If e'er thou look'dst on majesty.

Messenger She creeps.
Her motion and her station are as one.
She shows a body rather than a life,
A statue than a breather.

Cleopatra   Is this certain?

Messenger Or I have no observance.

Charmian   Three in Egypt
Cannot make better note.

Carel Press Carlisle,   www.carelpress.com

ACT THREE

Women of Words

Cleopatra	He's very knowing; I do perceive't. There's nothing in her yet. The fellow has good judgment.
Charmian	Excellent.
Cleopatra	Guess at her years, I prithee.
Messenger	Madam, She was a widow –
Cleopatra	Widow? Charmian, hark.
Messenger	And I do think she's thirty.
Cleopatra	Bear'st thou her face in mind? Is't long or round?
Messenger	Round even to faultiness.
Cleopatra	For the most part, too, they are foolish that are so. Her hair, what colour?
Messenger	Brown, madam: and her forehead As low as she would wish it.
Cleopatra	There's gold for thee. Thou must not take my former sharpness ill: I will employ thee back again; I find thee Most fit for business.

(Act 3, Scene 3)

In stage productions, at the point where the messenger says, "And I do think she's thirty." Cleopatra often briefly pauses before delivering her next line, and the audience usually laughs. Why do you think this is?

As a class, discuss what kind of woman you think Cleopatra is. Bear in mind that you have only had a 'taste' of what she is really like. Although you might have been amused by this selection remember that in the play she is a noble and tragic character. Ultimately, when Antony dies and she is without his protection, she is 'captured' by Caesar. She kills herself rather than live as a prisoner and without Antony.

From Much Ado About Nothing

ACT THREE

Women of Words

BEATRICE

Beatrice in *Much Ado About Nothing* is a clever woman who slightly terrifies everyone with her sharpness. She has been brought up in her uncle's house, and provides a striking contrast to her much more traditional and milder cousin called Hero. She is unusual for Shakespeare's times for the equality she demands for herself, and especially for her wit and intellect.

Her uncle, Leonato, tries to encourage her to get married, not because he wants rid of her, but because he believes it is the best for young women of her age. For example in Act 2 Scene 1 he says:

Leonato   By my troth, niece, thou wilt never get thee a husband if thou be so shrewd of thy tongue.

When her uncle says that he hopes she will one day be "fitted with a husband", she makes a typical sharp reply:

Beatrice   Not till God make men of some other metal than earth. Would it not grieve a woman to be over-mastered with a piece of valiant dust, to make an account of her life to a clod of wayward marl? No, uncle, I'll none: Adam's sons are my brethren; and truly, I hold it a sin to match in my kindred.

In addition to this example, Beatrice is frequently discussed by others for her sharpness. They see her as very unusual and, describe her, for example, as "My dear Lady Disdain", or "In faith, she's too curst", or "she speaks poinards and every word is stabs". Her wit and cleverness are a constant source of discussion among her friends and family.

Carel Press Carlisle,   www.carelpress.com

ACT THREE

Women of Words

marks = to take notice of

Courtesy ... presence = even courtesy herself would be rude to you

dear happiness = great good luck

scape ... face = escape getting his face scratched

parrot-teacher = great chatterer

BEATRICE FOR BENEDICK

Beatrice has for some time been feuding in fun with Benedick who is a popular young lord from Padua. They constantly tease and abuse each other in sharp-witted language which sometimes comes very close to the bone. Some of the most entertaining scenes in the play are the verbal jousting which goes on between them. Here are some examples:

Benedick has just returned from the wars and is greeting his friends when Beatrice notices him.

Beatrice: I wonder that you will still be talking, Signior Benedick; nobody marks you.

Benedick: What, my dear Lady Disdain! Are you yet living?

Beatrice: Is it possible disdain should die while she hath such meet food to feed it as Signior Benedick? Courtesy itself must convert to disdain if you come in her presence.

Benedick: Then is courtesy a turncoat. But it is certain I am loved of all ladies, only you excepted; and I would I could find in my heart that I had not a hard heart, for truly, I love none.

Beatrice: A dear happiness to women! They would else have been troubled with a pernicious suitor. I thank God and my cold blood, I am of your humour for that; I had rather hear my dog bark at a crow than a man swear he loves me.

Benedick: God keep your ladyship still in that mind! So some gentleman or other shall scape a predestinate scratched face.

Beatrice: Scratching could not make it worse, an 'twere such a face as yours were.

Benedick: Well, you are a rare parrot-teacher.

Beatrice: A bird of my tongue is better than a beast of yours

Benedick: I would my horse had the speed of your tongue ...

(Act I, Scene 1)

Carel Press Carlisle,   www.carelpress.com

There is another example of their exchange of insults and jokes. This one occurs at a masked ball organised to celebrate the safe return of the Duke's soldiers from war. In this instance, although they are supposed to be in disguise and unrecognisable to each other because of the masks they are wearing, both Beatrice and Benedick have recognised each other but are pretending that they haven't.

Beatrice Will you not tell me who told you so?

Benedick No, you shall pardon me.

Beatrice Nor will you not tell me who you are?

Benedick Not now.

Beatrice That I was disdainful, and that I had my good wit out of the "Hundred Merry Tales" – well, this was Signior Benedick that said so.

Benedick What's he?

Beatrice I am sure you know him well enough.

Benedick Not I, believe me.

Beatrice Did he never make you laugh?

Benedick I pray you, what is he?

Beatrice Why, he is the Prince's jester, a very dull fool; only his gift is in devising impossible slanders. None but libertines delight in him, and the commendation is not in his wit, but in his villainy; for he both pleases men and angers them, and then they laugh at him and beat him. I am sure he is in the fleet: I would he had boarded me.

Benedick When I know the gentleman, I'll tell him what you say.

Beatrice Do, do, he'll but break a comparison or two on me, which, peradventure not marked or not laughed at, strikes him into melancholy, and then there's a partridge wing saved, for the fool will eat no supper that night.

[Music]

We must follow the leaders.

Benedick In every good thing.

Beatrice Nay, if they lead to any ill, I will leave them at the next turning.

(Act 2, Scene 1)

The Hundred Merry Tales = was a well known book of jokes

libertines = good for nothings

fleet = company or crowd of people

but break a comparison = just make a few smart remarks

partridge wing = just a tiny piece

Carel Press Carlisle,   www.carelpress.com

ACT THREE

Women of Words

PRODUCTION ACTIVITY

Prepare for a performance of one of these scenes to the rest of the class. Divide into small groups and first, as a group, go through the language carefully to make sure you have understood the extent of the jokes and trade of insults. You might need to use the notes provided to help with some of the Shakespearian slang and colloquial language. Your teacher will help to interpret the text as well. You might like to think of what some of these expressions would be in today's slang.

Choose two actors to play the roles, and the rest of the group should help to work out how it would be best performed. Remember, you want to play the scene for as many laughs and clever insults as you can. These two characters, especially Beatrice, really enjoy the slinging of insults at each other.

Perform the scenes to the class. Discuss the performances, comparing the different interpretations given by different actors and the ways in which the humour has been brought out.

In these examples of the battle of jokes and traded insults between Beatrice and Benedick which of the two characters scores the most points over the other? Who do you think is the wittier and more clever?

***

Another of Shakespeare's comic plays also has a woman character famous for her blunt speaking and independent behaviour, especially in relation to men. Do you know which one it is? It is a play which has contributed a lot of negative language and jokes about strong women.

In the relations between the sexes today how much is it acceptable for a woman to be sharpwitted in the company of men? Do we accept women who are more clever than men? Think about these issues in relation to famous people such as male political leaders and their partners, as well as in your relations with members of the opposite sex.

By the way, this play *Much Ado About Nothing* is one of Shakespeare's most famous comedies, so as well as having lots of comic scenes in it, it also has a happy ending. Part of its happy ending is that Beatrice and Benedick, with a little help from their friends, eventually fall in love and get married. Would you have expected this from what you have seen of the two characters so far? You might ask your teacher to show you some scenes from the Kenneth Branagh film of the play if you want to know more about how this comes to pass.

The Epilogue

Willworks has been written to give you a taste of Shakespeare's talents, an introduction to his many stories and characters, a look at his skills as an entertainer and teller of mysterious tales. Through his words he continues to live in our culture even though he died four hundred years ago. Often people ask why we should still study Shakespeare and see his plays and how his work could still be relevant in today's world. Do you have any answers to these questions?

Perhaps you could end this unit of work with a class debate or discussion on the value to be gained from a study of Shakespeare's life and works. Use this as the basis for an essay on the same topic.

WHAT HAPPENS TO OPHELIA

Hamlet has killed Polonius, the father of Laertes and Ophelia. He has also cruelly rejected Ophelia. Here Laertes, still mourning his father, sees the effect on his sister. King Claudius sees the opportunity to use Laertes against Hamlet.

Laertes	How now, what noise is that? *(Ophelia enters)* O heat dry up my brains! Tears seven times salt Burn out the sense and virtue of mine eye! By heaven, thy madness shall be paid by weight Till our scale turns the beam. O rose of May, Dear maid, kind sister, sweet Ophelia! O heavens, is 't possible a young maid's wits Should be as mortal as an old man's life? Nature is fine in love, and where 'tis fine It sends some precious instance of itself After the thing it loves.
Ophelia	*(sings)* They bore him barefaced on the bier, Hey non nony, nony, hey nony, And on his grave rained many a tear— Fare you well, my dove.
Laertes	Hadst thou thy wits and didst persuade revenge, It could not move thus.
Ophelia	You must sing "Down, a-down", and you, "Call him a-down-a". O, how the wheel becomes it! It is the false steward that stole his master's daughter.
Laertes	This nothing's more than matter.
Ophelia	There's rosemary, that's for remembrance. Pray, love, remember. And there is pansies; that's for thoughts.
Laertes	A document in madness—thoughts and remembrance fitted.
Ophelia	There's fennel for you, and columbines. There's rue for you, and here's some for me. We may call it herb-grace o' Sundays. O, you must wear your rue with a difference. There's a daisy. I would give you some violets, but they withered all when my father died. They say a made a good end. *(Sings)* For bonny sweet Robin is all my joy.
Laertes	Thought and affliction, passion, hell itself She turns to favour and to prettiness.
Ophelia	*(sings)* And will a not come again, And will a not come again? No, no, he is dead, Go to thy death-bed, He never will come again.

Carel Press Carlisle,   www.carelpress.com

His beard as white as snow,
All flaxen was his poll.
He is gone, he is gone,
And we cast away moan.
God 'a' mercy on his soul.
And of all Christian souls, I pray God. God b' wi' ye.
(Ophelia leaves)

Laertes   Do you see this, O God?

King Claudius   Laertes, I must commune with your grief,
Or you deny me right. Go but apart,
Make choice of whom your wisest friends you will,
And they shall hear and judge 'twixt you and me.
If by direct or by collateral hand
They find us touched, we will our kingdom give,
Our crown, our life, and all that we call ours,
To you in satisfaction. But if not,
Be you content to lend your patience to us,
And we shall jointly labour with your soul
To give it due content.

Laertes   Let this be so.
His means of death, his obscure burial—
No trophy, sword, nor hatchment o'er his bones,
No noble rite nor formal ostentation—
Cry to be heard, as 'twere from heaven to earth,
That I must call 't in question.

King Claudius   So you shall;
And where th' offence is, let the great axe fall.
I pray you go with me.

Carel Press Carlisle,   www.carelpress.com.

CLAUDIUS PLOTS TO KILL HAMLET

In this scene, King Claudius persuades Laertes to take revenge on Hamlet.

King Claudius	Now must your conscience my acquittance seal, And you must put me in your heart for friend, Sith you have heard, and with a knowing ear, That he which hath your noble father slain Pursued my life.
Laertes	It well appears. But tell me Why you proceeded not against these feats, So crimeful and so capital in nature, As by your safety, wisdom, all things else, You mainly were stirred up.

unsinewed = weak

conjunctive = joined

general gender = common people

King Claudius	O, for two special reasons, Which may to you perhaps seem much unsinewed, And yet to me they're strong. The Queen his mother Lives almost by his looks; and for myself— My virtue or my plague, be it either which— She's so conjunctive to my life and soul That, as the star moves not but in his sphere, I could not but by her. The other motive Why to a public count I might not go Is the great love the general gender bear him, Who, dipping all his faults in their affection, Would, like the spring that turneth wood to stone, Convert his guilts to graces; so that my arrows, Too slightly timbered for so loud a wind, Would have reverted to my bow again, And not where I had aimed them.
Laertes	And so have I a noble father lost, A sister driven into desp'rate terms, Who has, if praises may go back again, Stood challenger, on mount, of all the age For her perfections. But my revenge will come.
King Claudius	Break not your sleeps for that. You must not think That we are made of stuff so flat and dull That we can let our beard be shook with danger, And think it pastime. You shortly shall hear more. I loved your father, and we love ourself. And that, I hope, will teach you to imagine—

A messenger arrives with news that Hamlet has returned to Denmark. Claudius sees a chance to use Laertes' desire for revenge by setting up a fencing match between Laertes and Hamlet. He also has a second plan in case the first fails.

King Claudius	Laertes, was your father dear to you? Or are you like the painting of a sorrow, A face without a heart?
Laertes	Why ask you this?

Carel Press Carlisle,   www.carelpress.com

King Claudius   Not that I think you did not love your father,
But that I know love is begun by time,
And that I see, in passages of proof,
Time qualifies the spark and fire of it.
Hamlet comes back. What would you undertake
To show yourself your father's son in deed
More than in words?

Laertes   To cut his throat i' th' church.

King Claudius   No place indeed should murder sanctuarize.
Revenge should have no bounds. But, good Laertes,
Will you do this?—keep close within your chamber.
Hamlet returned shall know you are come home.
We'll put on those shall praise your excellence,
And set a double varnish on the fame
The Frenchman gave you; bring you, in fine, together,
And wager on your heads. He, being remiss,
Most generous, and free from all contriving,
Will not peruse the foils; so that with ease,
Or with a little shuffling, you may choose
A sword unbated, and, in a pass of practice,
Requite him for your father.

Laertes   I will do 't,
And for that purpose I'll anoint my sword.
I bought an unction of a mountebank
So mortal that, but dip a knife in it,
Where it draws blood no cataplasm so rare,
Collected from all simples that have virtue
Under the moon, can save the thing from death
That is but scratched withal. I'll touch my point
With this contagion, that if I gall him slightly,
It may be death.

King Claudius   Let's further think of this;
Weigh what convenience both of time and means
May fit us to our shape. If this should fail,
And that our drift look through our bad performance,
'Twere better not essayed. Therefore this project
Should have a back or second that might hold
If this should blast in proof. Soft, let me see.
We'll make a solemn wager on your cunnings ...
I ha 't! When in your motion you are hot and dry—
As make your bouts more violent to that end—
And that he calls for drink, I'll have prepared him
A chalice for the nonce, whereon but sipping,
If he by chance escape your venomed stuck,
Our purpose may hold there.—

*the fame the Frenchman
gave you = Laertes' skill has
been praised by a famous
French swordsman*

peruse = examine

foils = fencing swords

*unbated = without a
protected tip, so sharp*

unction = ointment

mortal = deadly

nonce = time, moment

HAMLET CONFRONTS HIS MOTHER

When Hamlet's mother tries to rebuke him for his behaviour, he confronts her about her marriage. Polonius is hiding behind a tapestry to overhear their conversation.

Hamlet	Now, mother, what's the matter?
Queen Gertrude	Hamlet, thou hast thy father much offended.
Hamlet	Mother, you have my father much offended.
Queen Gertrude	Come, come, you answer with an idle tongue.
Hamlet	Go, go, you question with a wicked tongue.
Queen Gertrude	Why, how now, Hamlet?
Hamlet	What's the matter now?
Queen Gertrude	Have you forgot me?
Hamlet	No, by the rood, not so. You are the Queen, your husband's brother's wife. But—would you were not so—you are my mother.
Queen Gertrude	Nay, then, I'll set those to you that can speak.
Hamlet	Come, come, and sit you down. You shall not budge. You go not till I set you up a glass Where you may see the inmost part of you.
Queen Gertrude	What wilt thou do? Thou wilt not murder me? Help, help, ho!
Polonius	*(behind the arras)* What ho! Help, help, help!
Hamlet	How now, a rat? Dead for a ducat, dead. *(He thrusts his sword through the arras)*
Polonius	O, I am slain!
Queen Gertrude	*(to Hamlet)* O me, what hast thou done?
Hamlet	Nay, I know not. Is it the King?
Queen Gertrude	O, what a rash and bloody deed is this!
Hamlet	A bloody deed—almost as bad, good-mother, As kill a king and marry with his brother.
Queen Gertrude	As kill a king?
Hamlet	Ay, lady, 'twas my word. *(To Polonius)* Thou wretched, rash, intruding fool, farewell. I took thee for thy better. Take thy fortune. Thou find'st to be too busy is some danger.— Leave wringing of your hands. Peace, sit you down, And let me wring your heart; for so I shall If it be made of penetrable stuff...
Queen Gertrude	What have I done, that thou dar'st wag thy tongue In noise so rude against me?
Hamlet	Such an act That blurs the grace and blush of modesty, Calls virtue hypocrite, takes off the rose

rood= cross

glass = mirror

arras = tapestry

ducat = coin

Carel Press Carlisle,   www.carelpress.com

From the fair forehead of an innocent love
And sets a blister there, makes marriage vows
As false as dicers' oaths...

Queen Gertrude Ay me, what act,
That roars so loud and thunders in the index?

Hamlet Look here upon this picture, and on this,
The counterfeit presentment of two brothers.
See what a grace was seated on this brow—
A combination and a form indeed
Where every god did seem to set his seal
To give the world assurance of a man.
This was your husband. Look you now what follows.
Here is your husband, like a mildewed ear
Blasting his wholesome brother. Have you eyes?
Could you on this fair mountain leave to feed,
And batten on this moor? Ha, have you eyes?
You cannot call it love, for at your age
The heyday in the blood is tame, it's humble,
And waits upon the judgement; and what judgement
Would step from this to this? What devil was 't
That thus hath cozened you at hood-man blind?
O shame, where is thy blush? Rebellious hell,
If thou canst mutine in a matron's bones,
To flaming youth let virtue be as wax
And melt in her own fire. Proclaim no shame
When the compulsive ardour gives the charge,
Since frost itself as actively doth burn,
And reason panders will.

Queen Gertrude O Hamlet, speak no more!
Thou turn'st mine eyes into my very soul,
And there I see such black and grainèd spots
As will not leave their tinct.

Hamlet Nay, but to live
In the rank sweat of an enseamèd bed,
Stewed in corruption, honeying and making love
Over the nasty sty—

Queen Gertrude O, speak to me no more!
These words like daggers enter in mine ears.
No more, sweet Hamlet.

Hamlet A murderer and a villain,
A slave that is not twenti'th part the tithe
Of your precedent lord, a vice of kings,
A cutpurse of the empire and the rule,
That from a shelf the precious diadem stole
And put it in his pocket—

Queen Gertrude No more.

Hamlet A king of shreds and patches—

The ghost of Hamlet's father enters the room to remind Hamlet of his main
purpose – to revenge himself on Claudius.

mutine = rebel

leave their tinct = lose their colour

tithe = tenth